A Rookie reader®

W9-BJU-120

Who Needs Friends?

Written by Christine Taylor-Butler
Illustrated by Susan Havice

Children's Press®
A Division of Scholastic Inc.
New York • Toronto • London • Auckland • Sydney
Mexico City • New Delhi • Hong Kong
Danbury, Connecticut

To my best friends: Ken, Alexis, and Olivia
—C.T.

To Charles, Johnny, and Kyle, who have
friends everywhere.
—S.H.

Reading Consultant

Eileen Robinson
Reading Specialist

Library of Congress Cataloging-in-Publication Data

Taylor-Butler, Christine.
  Who needs friends? / written by Christine Taylor-Butler ; illustrated by Susan Havice.
      p. cm. — (A rookie reader)
  Summary: A boy is pleasantly surprised that his friends remember his birthday.
  ISBN 0-516-24979-7 (lib. bdg.)   0-516-24997-5 (pbk.)
  [1. Birthdays—Fiction. 2. Friendship—Fiction.] I. Havice, Susan, ill. II. Title. III. Series.
  PZ7.T2189Who 2006
  [E]—dc22

                                                              2005016185

CHILDREN'S PRESS, and A ROOKIE READER®, and associated logos are trademarks and/or
registered trademarks of Scholastic Library Publishing. SCHOLASTIC and associated logos are
trademarks and/or registered trademarks of Scholastic Inc.
1 2 3 4 5 6 7 8 9 10 R 15 14 13 12 11 10 09 08 07 06

Today is my birthday.
No one remembered.

When Nia had a birthday,
I made a card in art class.

Nia forgot my birthday.
She did not make a card for me.

When Henri had a birthday,
I baked a batch of cupcakes.

Henri forgot my birthday.
He did not bake cupcakes for me.

When Jasmine had a birthday, I played a song for her on my kazoo.

Jasmine forgot my birthday.
She did not play a song for me.

When my teacher had a birthday, I picked flowers for her.

Maybe the teacher forgot my birthday. She did not pick flowers for me.

That's okay.
I can make my own birthday card.

I can bake my own
birthday cupcakes.

I can play my own birthday song.

I can pick my own birthday flowers

Who needs friends anyway?

Surprise!

Word List (53 Words)

(Words in **bold** are story words that are repeated throughout the text.)

a	Henri	on
anyway	her	one
art	**I**	**own**
bake	in	pick
baked	is	picked
batch	Jasmine	play
birthday	kazoo	played
can	made	remembered
card	make	she
class	maybe	song
cupcakes	**me**	surprise
did	**my**	teacher
flowers	needs	that's
for	Nia	the
forgot	no	today
friends	**not**	**when**
had	of	who
he	okay	

About the Author

Christine Taylor-Butler studied both Engineering and Art & Design at Massachusetts Institute of Technology. When she's not writing stories children, you'll find her buried in her mountain of books. She lives in Kar City, Missouri, with her husband, two daughters, and many black cats.

About the Illustrator

Susan Havice lives in Massachusetts with her husband who is a his teacher. If you visited her studio you would find drawers filled with cray paints, and colored pencils. You would also find piles of paper on shelves. Susan has costumes hanging on hooks ready to try on, too.